Table of Contents

Copyright 4

Introduction 5

Understanding Interior Design Fees 7

An Overview of Interior Design Pricing Methods..................... 8

    1. Hourly Charging Method 10

        Hourly Pricing Checklist................................ 13

    2. Fixed/Flat-Fee Pricing 15

        Flat Fee Pricing Checklist 17

    3. Percentage-Based Fees................................ 19

        Percentage Fee Checklist................................ 21

    4. Consultation-Only Charges................................ 22

        Consultation Pricing Checklist............................ 25

    5. Retainer-Based Fees 26

        Retainer Pricing Checklist................................ 28

    6. Hybrid Charging Models................................ 29

        Hybrid Pricing Checklist................................ 33

    7. Tiered Service Packages 35

        Tiered Pricing Checklist 38

    8. Digital and Remote Design Pricing................................ 40

        Digital and Remote Design Pricing Checklist 42

    9. Value-Based Pricing (Advanced Use) 44

        Value-Based Pricing Checklist 45

Pricing Method Comparison Overview................................ 48

Global Pricing Safeguards..68

    Pricing Red Flags Checklist 70

    Pricing Confidence and Boundary Checklist 72

    Scope and Deliverables Confirmation Checklist...75

Common Pricing Mistakes to Avoid............................81

Pricing Method Selection Worksheet 86

Conclusion 90

Disclaimer 92

How Interior Designers Charge for

for

Projects and Services

PAYMENT OPTIONS FOR INTERIOR DESIGN CLIENTS

[2nd Edition Revised]

Virginia I Smith

Copyright

Introduction

One of the most challenging aspects of starting an interior design business is knowing how to charge for your work. And trust me, many are uncertain about how to charge adequately.

Many beginner designers feel confident in their creativity and their design decisions, but they are unsure about pricing, discussing fees with clients, and structuring payments professionally.

This book was written to remove that uncertainty and help those who truly don't know how to charge.

How Interior Designers Charge for Projects and Services is a practical, beginner-focused guide that explains the most common and modern pricing methods used in the interior design industry today.

It breaks down each option, clearly explaining when to use it, and also provides simple numerical examples, so you understand how fees are calculated in real situations.

The goal of this book is to show you that there is not just one way, or the right way to charge. You will find the available pricing options and choose the best methods that suit your experience level, project type, and business goals.

Understanding Interior Design Fees

Interior design fees are influenced by the level of the designer's expertise, the scope of the project, the location, and the type of service offered.

If you are a beginner in the industry, your priority should be clarity rather than complexity, as clients respond better to simple explanations and transparent pricing structures than to complex explanations with fancy language.

Charging properly for a service is not about charging the highest possible amount, but about charging fairly, covering your time and costs, and delivering value professionally in a sustainable way.

An Overview of Interior Design Pricing Methods

There are no fixed rules that dictate how interior design services must be priced. The most appropriate charging method depends on a combination of factors, including project scope, level of responsibility, and the designer's role. Because no two projects are identical, a single pricing approach is rarely suitable for every situation.

Choosing the right charging method is a strategic business decision. Even the strongest design concept can become difficult to deliver if the pricing structure does not adequately support the scope of work or the time required to execute it professionally.

The following list outlines the most common charging methods used in interior design practice today. Each option is presented in the order listed below and explained in detail in the sections that follow, helping designers understand when, how, and why each pricing method is applied. The charging methods covered in this book are:

1. Hourly Charging Method

2. Fixed / Flat Fee Pricing

3. Percentage-Based Fees

4. Consultation-Only Pricing

5. Retainer-Based Fees

6. Hybrid Charging Models

7. Tiered Service Packages

8. Digital and Remote Design Pricing

9. Value-Based Pricing (Use With Care)

1. **Hourly Charging Method**

Hourly pricing is one of the most commonly used charging methods in interior design, particularly for consultations, advisory services, and projects with uncertain duration.

Here, the designer charges a fixed rate for every hour spent executing a project, including time spent at meetings, site visits, design development, product sourcing, coordination, and revisions.

This method is often recommended for beginners because it is straightforward to calculate and easy to explain.

Some clients dislike the hourly rate, for obvious reasons; however, the fee-charging system is widely used by experienced professionals for specific project phases or limited engagements where flexibility is required.

Benefits

- It is transparent and easy for clients to understand.

- It reduces risk when a project scope is unclear.

- It is suitable for client consultations, troubleshooting, and short-term engagements.

- It allows designers to be compensated for all the time spent, from consulting with clients to driving while sourcing products.

Limitations

- Scalability is limited because income is directly tied to the amount of time spent.

- Clients may (usually do) question how time is spent.

- Inefficient workflows can reduce profitability.

Example:

If your hourly rate is $75 and you work 24 hours on a project:

$75 \times 24 = \$1,800$

For professionals, hourly pricing is best supported by time tracking systems and clearly defined billable activities.

Hourly Pricing Checklist

When TO Use Hourly Pricing

Use this method when:

- The project scope is unclear or still evolving.

- The client needs ongoing advice or revisions.

- The project timeline is flexible.

- You can track time accurately.

Before quoting (tick):

- Hourly rate confirmed.

- Billable activities defined.

- Time tracking method selected.

- Billing frequency agreed on (weekly or monthly).

When NOT to Use Hourly Pricing

- When the client wants a fixed total cost.

- When the scope is clearly defined.

- When the client questions time spent.

- When efficiency can reduce your income.

2. Fixed/Flat-Fee Pricing

Flat-fee pricing involves charging a single, predetermined amount for a clearly defined scope of work. This method is widely used in residential and commercial interior design projects where deliverables can be reasonably predicted.

Flat fees require experience and detailed scope definition. While beginners can use this method for smaller projects, professionals often rely on it for full-service turnkey design work.

Benefits

- The designer's income is predicted from the onset.

- There is cost certainty for the client. Not a penny more, not a penny less.

- It encourages efficient workflows.

- It is a commonly accepted charging method in professional practice.

Limitations

- There is a risk of under-pricing if the scope of work is poorly defined.

- Requires strong contracts and boundaries.

- Scope creeping up can adversely affect profitability.

Example:

A designer charges a flat fee of $6,000 for a full living room redesign. This covers concept development, drawings, product sourcing, and project coordination.

Professionals often calculate flat fees based on estimated hours multiplied by a determined hourly rate, plus contingency.

Flat Fee Pricing Checklist

When TO Use Flat Fees

Use this method when:

- The project scope and deliverables are clearly defined.

- Revision limits are set (at the initial stage).

- The timeline is predictable.

- You can estimate hours spent confidently.

Before quoting (tick):

- ○ Scope written and agreed upon.

- ○ Deliverables listed.

- ○ Revision limits stated.

- ○ Exclusions are clearly noted.

When NOT to Use Flat Fees

- When the scope of work is likely to change.

- When the client is indecisive.

- When the project's complexity is unknown.

- When the designer's experience level is still very limited.

3. Percentage-Based Fees

Percentage-based fees are calculated as a percentage of the total project cost. The pricing method is commonly used in full-service interior design projects. Aside from the creative aspect, the designer is involved in coordination, specification, and overall project delivery.

This pricing approach works best for larger projects with clearly defined budgets and experienced designers who can manage both scope and client expectations.

Benefits

- It scales naturally with project size and degree of complexity.
- Reflects the level of responsibility involved.

- It is commonly accepted in professional practice.

- Suitable for full-service and high-budget projects.

Limitations

- The final fee depends on the total project cost.

- Less predictable at early project stages.

- It may raise transparency concerns if not explained clearly to clients.

Example:

Project budget: $120,000

Design fee at 10% = $12,000

Percentage-based pricing works best when the scope is clearly defined, and the designer explains exactly what costs the percentage applies to.

Percentage Fee Checklist

When TO Use Percentage Fees

Use this method when:

- A project budget is established.

- You are involved in project coordination and products procurement.

- The project size justifies the ongoing involvement.

- The client understands the percentage billing system.

Before quoting (tick):

- o Percentage clearly stated.

- o All costs included/excluded are defined.

- o Budget reference is confirmed.

- o Transparency aspect explained to client.

When NOT to Use Percentage Fees

- When the budget is unknown.

- For low-budget projects.

- For advice-only services.

- When client distrusts or is uncomfortable with the percentage pricing.

4. Consultation-Only Charges

Consultation-only pricing involves charging a fixed fee for professional advice, without ongoing design responsibility.

Here, the designer provides guidance, recommendations, and direction, but does not manage project implementation.

This charging method is suitable for both beginners and professionals who offer short-term or introductory services.

Benefits

- Clear boundaries and limited commitment.

- Easy to price and deliver.

- Ideal for first-time clients.

- Low risk for both designer and client.

Limitations

- It has a limited income potential.

- The designer has no control over the project's outcome.

- The designer's advice may not be implemented correctly.

Example:

$200 for a two-hour in-home or virtual consultation.

Consultation-only services work best when the scope is clearly stated and the designer documents recommendations in writing.

Consultation Pricing Checklist

When TO Use Consultation-Only Pricing

Use this method when:

- Client wants only advice services.

- No ongoing responsibility is required.

- Work scope is short and defined.

- Project implementation is client-led.

Before quoting (tick):

- o Duration confirmed.
- o Deliverables clarified.
- o Responsibility limits stated.
- o Notes or follow-up agreed on.

When NOT to Use Consultation-Only Pricing

- When the client expects ongoing support.

- When implementation control is required.

- When the project's complexity is high.

- When advice may be misapplied.

5. Retainer-Based Fees

A retainer is an upfront payment that secures a designer's time and availability over a mutually agreed period.

It is commonly used for long-term, phased, or ongoing residential and commercial interior design projects.

Retainers help stabilise cash flow and signal serious client commitment.

Benefits

- Improves cash flow.

- Secures the client's commitment.

- Suitable for ongoing or work carried out in phases.

- Reduces payment delays

Limitations

- Requires a clear scope definition.

- It may deter budget-conscious clients.

- Needs careful tracking and documentation.

Example:

A monthly retainer of $5,000 covering agreed advisory and coordination services.

Retainer-based pricing works best when the duration, services covered, and billing terms are clearly outlined, in writing.

Retainer Pricing Checklist

When TO Use Retainers Fee

Use this method when:

- The work/tasks span months or split in phases.

- The client needs regular access.

- The scope is ongoing but bounded.

- Cash flow stability is important.

Before quoting (tick):

- o Monthly fee set.

- o Hours/services included defined.

- o Duration stated clearly.

- o Excesses addressed.

When NOT to Use Retainers

- For one-off projects.

- When design scope is unclear.

- When the client resists upfront payment.

- Without written contract agreements.

6. Hybrid Charging Models

Hybrid pricing is using more than one charging method within the same project.

Instead of relying on a single pricing structure, the designer combines two or more methods that better cover the scope, timeline, and amount of responsibility involved.

This approach works well because interior design projects often change as they progress. Early stages may require fixed pricing, while later stages may require flexibility to accommodate revisions, site issues, additional client requests, etc...

Benefits

- Provides pricing clarity while allowing flexibility.

- Reduces the risk of undercharging.

- Adapts well to complex or phased projects.

- Supports fair compensation across varied tasks.

Limitations

- Requires a clear explanation to clients.

- Needs strong written documentation.

- It can feel complicated for inexperienced designers.

- Poorly defined boundaries can lead to tension.

Examples:

1. **Consultation + Flat Fee:** A designer charges a consultation fee for initial advice, followed by a fixed fee for a defined design package.

- **Flat Fee + Hourly:** A flat fee covers core design services. Additional revisions, site visits, or changes are billed at hourly rates.

- **Retainer + Hourly:** A client pays a monthly retainer to secure the designer's availability. Extra work is billed at an hourly rate.

- **Percentage + Flat Fee:** A flat fee is charged for design development, with a percentage applied to procurement or project coordination.

Setting firm fees where possible, while charging separately for unpredictable additional work outside the original scope, reduces the risk of undercharging. It also helps prevent disputes over what is included (or not) in the fee.

Hybrid Pricing Checklist

When TO Use Hybrid Pricing

Use this method when:

- A project has mixed certainty levels.

- Some phases are defined, others open-ended.

- You want flexibility with added protection.

Before quoting (tick):

- ○ Each pricing component is explained.

- ○ Boundaries are clearly stated.

- ○ Documentation is detailed.

When NOT to Use Hybrid Pricing

- When client prefers simplicity.

- When communication between parties is weak.

- Without strong contracts.

- If you're new to pricing for interior design services.

7. Tiered Service Packages

Tiered service packages offer clients a set of clearly defined services at different price points. Each includes a specific scope of work, allowing clients to choose the option that best fits their needs and budget.

This pricing method works well for designers who offer repeatable services, such as residential or digital design, where deliverables can be standardised.

Benefits

- Gives clients clear, easy-to-compare options.

- Reduces negotiation and price uncertainties.

- Helps designers work more efficiently.

- Encourages clients to upgrade to higher tiers.

Limitations

- Less flexible for highly customised projects.

- Requires very clear scope definitions.

- Not ideal for complex or unpredictable workflows.

Example:

Basic tier: $1,200

- Concept design, mood board, and general guidance.

Standard tier: $2,500

- Concept design, layout suggestions, product selections, and limited revisions.

Premium: $4,500

- Full design development, detailed drawings, sourcing support, and ongoing coordination.

Each tier clearly states what is included and excludes services outside the package scope, which can be billed separately.

Tiered service packages work best when each level is clearly documented and communicated. When structured carefully, they simplify pricing, improve client decision-making, and support consistent, scalable services.

Tiered Pricing Checklist

When TO Use Tiered Packages

Use this method when:

- Services are repeatable.

- Deliverables can be standardised.

- Clients have varied budgets.

Before quoting (tick):

- Each tier is clearly defined.

- Inclusions/exclusions are stated.

- Upgrade paths are well-explained.

When NOT to Use Tiered Packages

- For highly customised projects.

- When the scope varies widely.

- When client needs bespoke solutions.

8. Digital and Remote Design Pricing

Digital and remote design pricing applies to interior design services delivered online without in-person site visits. Designers provide concepts, layouts, product selections, and guidance to their online clients using digital tools and communication platforms.

This method allows designers to work with clients worldwide and is commonly used for smaller projects, room interiors, or advice-based consultation services.

Benefits

- Minimal overheads and zero travel costs.

- Allows designers to work remotely with a wider range of clientele (beyond the locals).

- Faster turnaround for defined services.

- Scalable for repeatable offerings.

Limitations

- Limited to zero control over on-site works.

- Relies heavily on clients for measurements and other detailed information.

- Not suitable for complex renovations and interior installations.

Example:

$750 per room for a complete virtual design package.

Digital pricing only works best when deliverables are clearly defined, and client expectations are carefully managed.

Clear instructions and documentation are essential to avoid misunderstandings between both parties.

Digital and Remote Design Pricing Checklist

When TO Use Digital Pricing

Use this method when:

- All services are delivered online.

- Site visits are unnecessary or not possible.

- Deliverables are clearly defined.

Before quoting (tick):

- Client input requirements are listed.

- Service limitations are stated.

- Digital deliverables are confirmed.

When NOT to Use Digital Pricing

- For complex renovations and interior construction.

- When the site conditions significantly affect design decisions.

- When the client cannot provide accurate measurements or visuals.

9. Value-Based Pricing (Advanced Use)

Value-based pricing fees are based on the value of the outcome rather than the time spent on it or the total project cost. The designer charges based on the impact the design is expected to have on the client, such as increased usability, brand presence, or higher revenue potential.

This pricing method is best suited for experienced designers with proven results and strong client trust.

Benefits

- Higher earning potential.

- Focuses on results rather than the hours spent on a project.

- Not limited by time-based pricing.

Limitations

- Difficult to justify without long-term experience.

- Requires strong client confidence.

- Risky, if the value is unclear (or subjective).

Example

Charging $15,000 for a retail redesign that is expected to improve customer flow and sales.

Value-based pricing should be used selectively, be supported by clear goals, and must have measurable outcomes. It can lead to misaligned expectations without proper experience.

Value-Based Pricing Checklist

When TO Use Value-Based Pricing

Use this method when:

- Outcomes matter more than hours expended.

- You have a proven professional experience.

- The client understands value-driven fees.

Before quoting (tick):

- o Value is clearly articulated

- o Outcomes are discussed and agreed upon

- o Expectations are aligned in writing

When NOT to Use Value-Based Pricing

- As a beginner.

- When outcomes are vague.

- When the client is highly price-focused.

- When trust and credibility are not established.

Pricing Method Comparison Overview

PRICING METHOD COMPARISON OVERVIEW

The table below provides a high-level comparison of common charging methods to help designers quickly identify suitable options based on project type and experience level.

Pricing Method	Best For	Risk Level	Beginner Friendly	Scalability
Hourly	Consultations, small talks, advice	Low	Yes	Low
Flat fee	Defined projects	Medium	Yes (small scope)	Medium
Percentage-based (%)	Full-service projects	Medium to high	Limited	High
Consultation only	Advice-based work	Low	Yes	Low
Retainer	Ongoing services	Medium	Moderate	Medium
Hybrid-models	Complex projects	Medium	Moderate	High
Tiered packages	Residential and commercial services	Low to medium	Yes	Medium
Digital/Remote	Virtual services	Low	Yes	Medium
Value based	Outcome-driven work	High	No	Very high

*** This overview highlights that no single pricing method suits every situation, and the best choice depends on project scope, experience level, and business goals.

Pricing Scenarios: Applying the Methods in Real Projects

This section shows how the pricing methods are used in realistic interior design situations. They cover scenarios from beginner-friendly residential projects to advanced commercial work.

SCENARIO 1: HOURLY CHARGING METHOD

Project Type: Advisory and design support.

Client: A homeowner renovating a small studio apartment.

Scope: Interior design advice, space-plan and layout suggestions, finishes guidance, product sourcing assistance.

Level of uncertainty: Medium to high.

Why choose hourly pricing?

At the outset, the client had a general idea of what they wanted but there was no fixed brief, no confirmed budget, and an evolving timeline.

The designer anticipated there will be ongoing discussions, revisions, and decision-making support, rather than a clearly defined deliverable.

Hourly pricing was selected to ensure the designer would be compensated fairly for all time spent, regardless of how the project evolved.

Pricing structure

Hourly rate: $75 per hour.
Billable activities:

- Client meetings.

- Design development.

- Research and sourcing.

- Revisions (if any).

- Communication and coordination time.

Time spent was tracked and invoiced weekly.

Fee calculation

Total hours worked: 28hrs

$28 \times 75 = \underline{\textbf{\$2,100}}$

Outcome

The client appreciated the flexibility of paying only for time used, and the designer avoided the risk of under cutting and under-pricing an open-ended project. This method worked well because expectations were clearly communicated and time tracking was transparent.

Hourly pricing is effective when the scope is fluid, and when both parties understand that additional time equals additional fees.

SCENARIO 2: FIXED/FLAT-FEE PRICING

Project Type: A two-bedroom residential redesign.

Client: Homeowner with a clear brief on their requirements.

Scope: Concept design, space-plan, finishes selection, furniture list, and two revisions.

Level of uncertainty: Low.

Why was flat-fee pricing chosen?

Because the client had a clearly defined goal, timeline, and budget, things were clear and straightforward. The designer was confident in estimating the time and deliverables required to complete the project successfully.

Also, a flat fee was chosen to give the client cost certainty and allow the designer to work efficiently, without tracking every hour.

Pricing structure

Estimated internal time: 22 hours.

Internal target rate: $75 per hour.

Calculation used internally:

$22 \times 75 = \$1,650$

Fixed fee quoted to client: **$1,750**

Outcome

The client knew the total cost upfront and felt comfortable committing to the project. The designer completed the work within the estimated time and retained full control over the entire workflow.

Fixed pricing works best when the scope is clearly defined and revision limits are agreed upon in advance.

SCENARIO 3: PERCENTAGE-BASED FEE

Project Type: Residential renovation works

Client: A homeowner undertaking a multi-room renovation project.

Scope: Space planning, finishes, fixtures, furnishings, sourcing, and project coordination.

Level of uncertainty: Medium.

Why was percentage-based pricing chosen?

The project involved multiple phases, a substantial budget, and ongoing coordination with suppliers, contractors, and installers. As the project progresses, the designer's level of responsibility increases. So, to ensure compensation scaled appropriately with project size and complexity the percentage-based fee was chosen.

Pricing structure

Total project budget: $120,000

Design fee percentage: 10%

Calculation:

120,000 × 10% = **$12,000**

The percentage applied to construction and furnishings costs only, as clearly stated in the agreement.

Outcome

As the project evolved, the designer's compensation remained aligned with the scope and responsibility involved. The client understood how the fee was calculated and appreciated the transparency.

Percentage-based pricing works best when budgets are clearly defined and when the designer explains exactly what costs the percentage applies to.

SCENARIO 4: CONSULTATION-ONLY CHARGES

Project Type: Interior design advice and direction only.

Client: A homeowner seeking professional guidance on interior design works in a new house.

Scope: Layout advice, colour recommendations, furniture placement, window treatments, and an outdoor leisure room design.

Level of uncertainty: Low (short engagement).

Why consultation-only pricing was chosen

The client did not need ongoing design services and preferred to implement changes independently. The designer's role was limited to providing professional advice within a fixed time frame.

Consultation-only pricing allowed both parties to engage with clear scopes and boundaries, with minimal commitment.

Pricing structure

Consultation duration: 3 hours

Flat consultation fee: **$500**

The designer provided verbal guidance during the session and followed up with brief written notes, and detailed documentation to help guide the client.

Outcome

The client received professional direction without committing to a full interior design service while the designer delivered value efficiently, avoiding responsibility for project implementation.

Consultation-only pricing works best when the scope is clearly limited and the designer documents recommendations to avoid misunderstandings.

SCENARIO 5: RETAINER-BASED FEES

Project Type: An ongoing commercial renovation support.

Client: A business owner managing a phased dental office renovation.

Scope: Design advice, drawings review, supplier coordination, site check-instructions.

Level of uncertainty: Medium to high (long timeline).

Why retainer pricing was chosen

The project was spread over several months with no fixed end date and the client required regular access to the interior designer, rather than a one-off design delivery.

A retainer was chosen to secure availability while ensuring predictable income. This approach allowed the designer to support the project without repeatedly renegotiating design fees.

Pricing structure

Monthly retainer: $2,000

Duration: 3 months.

Calculation:

2,000 × 4 = **$8,000**

The agreement clearly stated the number of hours
and services covered per month, with additional
work billed separately.

Outcome

The designer maintained steady cash flow, and the
client had consistent professional support.
Retainer pricing worked well because
expectations, time limits, and responsibilities were
clearly defined from the start.

SCENARIO 6: HYBRID CHARGING MODEL

Project Type: Commercial interior design project.

Client: A small business owner opening a boutique café.

Scope: Concept design, space planning, finishes, procurement support, site coordination.

Level of uncertainty: Medium.

Why was hybrid pricing chosen?

Some project phases were clearly defined, while others depended on construction progress and approvals. A hybrid model balanced structure with flexibility. The designer combined a flat-fee for design development with a percentage-based fee for procurement and project coordination.

Pricing structure

Flat design fee: $7,000

Fit-out budget: $200,000

Percentage fee: 6%

Calculation:

200,000 × 6% = $12,000

Total fee: **$19,000**

Outcome

The designer was fairly compensated for both creative work and ongoing involvement. The client also understood the price breakdown, which reduced friction between both parties while the project was ongoing.

Hybrid pricing works best when each component is clearly explained and documented.

SCENARIO 7: TIERED SERVICE PACKAGES

Project Type: Residential design services.

Client: Homeowners with varying budgets.

Scope: Predefined service packages.

Level of uncertainty: Low.

Why tiered pricing was chosen

The designer offered repeatable services that could be standardised. Tiered packages simplified decision-making and reduced the need for custom quotes.

Clients selected a package based on their budget and designer's involvement level.

Pricing structure

Basic Package: **$1,200** (concept + guidance)

Standard Package: **$2,500** (design + sourcing)

Premium Package: **$4,500** (full design + coordination)

Outcome

Clients appreciated having clear options, and the designer increased efficiency by repeating similar workflows. Tiered pricing worked best because each package had clearly defined inclusions and exclusions.

SCENARIO 8: DIGITAL AND REMOTE DESIGN PRICING

Project Type: Virtual walk-through apartment room designs.

Client: A remote homeowner (thousands of miles away).

Scope: Online consultation, layout plan, mood board, shopping list.

Level of uncertainty: Low.

Why digital pricing was chosen

The client required only professional input from the designer miles away (without in-person visits). Deliverables were clearly defined and delivered seamlessly through digital technology.

A flat digital fee allows an efficient workflow while a designer can work with any client globally (geographic flexibility).

Pricing structure

Digital design fee: **$750 per room**

The agreement specified required client inputs, like rough sketches with measurements, and photos to show as many details as was needed by the designer.

Outcome

The designer delivered a complete service remotely with minimal overhead. Digital pricing worked best because expectations, limitations, and deliverables were clearly documented.

SCENARIO 9: VALUE-BASED PRICING

Project Type: Commercial workspace redesign.

Client: Professional services firm.

Scope: Space optimisation, brand alignment, client experience, general improvement

Level of uncertainty: High (outcome-driven).

Why value-based pricing was chosen

The client's priority was not about hours spent, but the business impact. The redesign was expected to improve workflow efficiency, staff satisfaction, and client perception.

The designer priced the service based on the anticipated value rather than scope, time spent, or project cost.

Pricing structure

Value-based fee: **$25,000**

The fee was justified through discussions about expected outcomes and long-term benefits.

Outcome

The designer was compensated for strategic professional expertise, rather than time spent. Value-based pricing worked because the client understood the benefits and trusted the designer's experience.

Global Pricing Safeguards

(The sections that follow apply to all the pricing methods discussed in this book.)

Regardless of which pricing method an interior designer chooses for a project, there are precautions to be applied consistently across all projects.

They are safeguards that exist to protect time, income, professional boundaries, and client relationships. They are not tied to any specific pricing structure, but to sound business practice.

Even a well-structured pricing method can fail if the first warning signs are ignored. Issues like:

- Unclear project scope.

- Mismatched expectations.

- Client's reluctance to discuss the budget.

- Unclear scope of work.

And more. They often lead to:

- Underpaid or even unpaid work.

- Strained communication between parties.

- Dissatisfaction.

- Designer's lethargy.

And worst scenario, rancour or litigation. With global pricing safeguards, designers can identify potential problems before being committed to any project.

Reviewing these before accepting any project is best, as they encourage informed decision-making rather than reactive pricing. They also allow designers, whether beginners or experienced professionals, assess risk objectively, communicate boundaries clearly, and enter contractual agreements confidently.

Pricing Red Flags Checklist

(Use Before Accepting Any Project)

The first and most important safeguard is recognising warning signs before accepting a project.

Not every prospect is a good one, even when it appears appealing, or the client expresses a strong interest in working with you. Pricing and project scope issues often reveal themselves early. Subtly, in most cases, but early. As a designer, the onus lies on you to look out for small but consistent warning signs.

Identifying the following red flags before signing any agreement or moving to the project site will prevent costly disputes and protect long-term professional reputation.

The checklist below is designed to help designers pause, assess, and decide whether a project is commercially viable and professionally sustainable (or not).

A single red flag on its own may not be a deal-breaker, but three or more? This often indicates future challenges with pricing, scope control, or client expectations.

Use this checklist before committing to a client, or most importantly, finalising fees. Notice when a prospective client:

1. Avoids discussing the budget.

2. Expects unlimited revisions.

3. Resists a written contract agreement.

4. Requests for (unpaid) extras.

5. Downplays the professional value.

6. Compares you to others on price rather than competence.

7. Pushes for deals or discounts immediately.

8. Gives an undefined scope or is constantly shifting/changing.

Multiple red flags like these often signal future pricing, boundary, and payment issues.

Pricing Confidence and Boundary Checklist

(Don't just assess the monetary figures.)

Before confirming interior design fees to charge or accepting a project, interior designers should assess not only the numbers but also their own confidence and boundaries around the work.

Pricing issues often arise not because the method is wrong, but because boundaries were unclear or confidence was compromised during early conversations.

This aspect of safeguarding helps designers pause and evaluate whether they are entering a project from a position of clarity and control, rather than urgency or pressure.

It is especially useful for beginners, but also relevant for experienced designers navigating complex or high-stakes projects.

Use this checklist before sending out proposals, quoting fees, or agreeing to revised scopes. Ask yourself the following questions honestly:

1. Am I confident explaining this pricing method without apologising or over-justifying?

2. Does this fee realistically cover my time and expertise?

3. Will it adequately cover the responsibilities I will provide?

4. Have I clearly defined what is included and what is not?

5. Do I feel pressured to lower my fee to secure the project?

6. Am I (only) relying on future upsells to make this project worthwhile?

7. Would I still accept this project if the client did not negotiate?

If hesitation appears repeatedly, it may indicate that the pricing method is unsuitable, the scope needs refinement, or the client may not be a good fit.

Confidence at the pricing stage often predicts smoother project delivery.

Scope and Deliverables Confirmation Checklist

(Review this before issuing agreements or invoices.)

Many pricing disputes stem from vague or assumed scope, rather than intentional conflict. So, use the checklist tool help you confirm that both you and the client share the same understanding of what will be delivered, regardless of how the project is priced.

Confirm that the following have been clearly stated. It should be reviewed again whenever the project scope changes:

- Services included in the fee.

- Services explicitly excluded.

- Number of design concepts provided.

- Number of revisions allowed.

- The format of all deliverables, like digital files, drawings, mood boards, vision charts, and other presentations.

- The level of project site involvement, if any.

- Sourcing and procurement responsibilities.

- Client responsibilities and response times.

- Payment milestones or billing frequency.

- The conditions under which the fee structure may change.

A clear scope definition (from the beginning) protects both the designer and the client. It also significantly reduces the risk of scope creep, unpaid or underpaid work, and misunderstandings.

Best Practices for Choosing and Applying Pricing Models

Selecting the right pricing model depends on the designer's experience, project scope, and risk tolerance. A pricing structure that works well for a small consultation may be unsuitable for a full-service renovation, just as a model appropriate for an experienced studio may be risky for a beginner to handle.

Understanding these variables allows designers to choose pricing methods that support both the project and their long-term sustainability.

If you are a beginner, you should prioritise manageable commitments and clearly defined services.

Simple pricing structures reduce confusion, help build confidence, and make it easier to communicate fees to clients. As experience grows, designers can gradually introduce more flexible and layered pricing structures that show increased responsibility, expertise, and project complexity.

Pricing for interior design services should support learning and growth, not create unnecessary pressure.

Clear documentation, written agreements, and scope definitions are essential, regardless of the pricing method used. These elements protect both the designer and the client, by setting expectations from the outset and reducing the likelihood of misunderstandings. Well-documented pricing also displays your professional credibility, and signals that you can operate professionally, with a well-put-in-place structure, and a focused intent.

Consistency in applying pricing policies is also important. Making frequent exceptions, discounting without reason, or adjusting fees informally can and will weaken boundaries and create confusion between the parties. Designers who apply their pricing methods consistently tend to experience smoother, better implemented projects, stronger client relationships, and fewer disputes.

Pricing should and will evolve with experience.

Regular reviews help ensure that fees remain aligned with skills, market conditions, and business goals. Reviewing completed projects allows designers to identify under-pricing, inefficiencies, or scope challenges, and to then learn to adjust future fees accordingly. A pricing model that once felt appropriate may no longer reflect the designer's value, as experience increases.

In the end, effective pricing is not only about numbers, but about clarity, confidence, and professionalism. When fee charging models are chosen thoughtfully and applied steadily, they support better project outcomes, healthier client relationships, and sustainable business growth.

Common Pricing Mistakes to Avoid

One of the most common pricing mistakes interior designers make is undercharging due to a lack of confidence or fear of losing a client.

1: Undercharging

While undercharging may secure getting a project in the short term, it often leads to overwork, resentment, and unsustainable business practices. Both beginners and professionals should remember that pricing communicates value and professionalism, not just cost.

2: Scope creep (when a project quietly expands but the price does not).

Another frequent mistake is failing to define the scope of work clearly. When services are not properly outlined and documented, clients may erroneously assume that what you call additional work is included in the bill. This leads to scope creep, unpaid hours, and strained relationships. Written agreements, clear deliverables, and defined revision limits are important safeguards against such.

3: Using a single-charge model

A third mistake is relying on just one pricing method for all projects. Different projects require different approaches, and designers who adapt their pricing to project type, complexity, and risk tend to achieve better outcomes and a more stable income.

4. Failing to Account for Time Beyond Design Work

Many designers calculate fees based only on visible design tasks and overlook the time spent on emails, meetings, revisions, coordination, sourcing, and follow-ups. Each task may appear minor, but they quickly accumulate and significantly affect a designer's profitability. Pricing should reflect the full scope of professional involvement and not just the creative output.

5. Not Charging for Revisions or Additional Requests

Another common mistake is paying no attention to revisions that creep in silently. Treating them as if they are nothing much to worry about while allowing additional requests without adjusting fees, is risky. When revision limits are not defined, clients may (and will) continue to request changes without understanding the designer's time input. Clearly stating what constitutes a revision and how additional work is billed helps protect both time and income.

6. Adjusting Fees Mid-Conversation, Without Review

Reducing fees during client discussions without reassessing the scope or expected deliverables can undermine professional credibility. Price changes should be deliberate. They must be based on a revised scope, not pressure or discomfort. Designers who pause, review, and respond formally tend to maintain stronger boundaries and clearer agreements.

7. Ignoring Early Warning Signs from Clients

Some designers proceed with projects despite clear warning signs, such as resistance to contracts, reluctance to discuss budget, or repeated comparisons based solely on price. Overlooking these sometimes-glaring indicators often leads to disputes, late payments, or dissatisfaction. Recognising and responding to early warning signs is a critical part of sustainable pricing practice.

Finally, avoiding these common pricing mistakes allows designers to protect their time, maintain professional boundaries, and build more sustainable and rewarding practices.

Pricing Method Selection Worksheet

[Use this template to help identify the most suitable pricing method for your project. Complete it before quoting any fee].

Project Name:

_____

Client Name:

_____

Location:

_____

Project Type (e.g. residential, commercial, digital-only):

_____

_____

Project Scope (rooms, size, complexity):

_____

_____

Client Type:

_____

Pricing Method(s):

_____

Fee Calculations:

_____

_____

_____

_____

_____

_____

_____

_____

_____

_____

_____

_____

_____

Notes:

Pricing Method Selection Worksheet

[Use this template to help identify the most suitable pricing method for your project. Complete it before quoting any fee].

Project Name:

_____

Client Name:

_____

Location:

_____

Project Type (e.g. residential, commercial, digital-only):

_____

_____

Project Scope (rooms, size, complexity):

_____

_____

Client Type:

_____

Pricing Method(s):

_____

Fee Calculations:

_____
_____
_____
_____
_____
_____
_____
_____
_____
_____
_____
_____
_____
_____

Notes:

Conclusion

Understanding how best to charge for interior design services is a critical professional skill that develops over time. There is no universal pricing model. Only methods that, more or less, depend on experience, project type, and business structure.

By understanding the strengths and limitations of each option, interior designers can make much better decisions that protect their income, support their workflow, and build trust with clients. With practice and confidence, pricing the right way will no longer be a source of anxiety, but a strategic tool for a business's sustainable growth.

Charging for interior design services does not have to be confusing or intimidating. With clear methods, honest communication, and realistic expectations, every designer can build sustainable pricing systems.

This book provides a foundation for understanding common and modern charging options. As experience grows, designers can refine and adapt these methods to suit their practice. Professional pricing supports better projects, stronger client relationships, good profits, and long-term career growth.

Disclaimer

This book is intended for informational and educational purposes only.

The content does not constitute legal, financial, accounting, or business advice.

Interior design fees, contracts, and business practices vary widely, depending on location, experience level, project type, and local regulations.

Readers are responsible for conducting their own research and seeking professional advice where appropriate, including legal and financial guidance, before implementing any pricing structures or business decisions discussed in this book. The author makes no guarantees regarding income, profitability, or business success.

By using the information in this book, the reader acknowledges that all business decisions are made at their own discretion and risk.

Random Notes Section

Random Notes Section